HIRAM
MORGAN HILL

by
Beth Wyman

*I hope you enjoy the
story of
"Mr." Morgan Hill.*

Beth Wyman

This book has been reproduced in the United States of
America. It is typeset by Four Star Communications,
printed by Jeda Publications and published by the author.

ISBN 0-9627098-9-1

Table of Contents

Acknowledgements................................... v

Introduction...ix

Hiram Morgan Hill.............................. 1

Diana Murphy Hill............................... 5

Diane Murphy-Hill...............................13

Sarah Althea Hill Sharon Terry.......33

Mary Ellen "Mammy" Pleasant.........53

The Morgan Hill Ranch Subdivision...........59

References.. 69

Acknowledgements

This work is dedicated to all of those who have gone before. For those who made the history and for those who kept the record. I am particularly indebted to the efforts of local scholars who tried to fathom the Murphy-Morgan Hill mystique and separate fact from fiction. The following have provided assistance, resources, and encouragement:

In Morgan Hill and Gilroy

Caecil Bradford Barrett
Olive Vivienne Palmer Belletto
Ida Costa Link
Norma Edes Link
Anita Kell Mason
Mary Frassetti Prien
Jean and Robert Rice
John Robertson
Catherine Tallman Bishop Stone
Leon and Richie Thomas
Adelaide Sharp Walgren
Jim Williams

In Elko

Terry Clark
Tom Clark
Orville Wilson

In Cape Girardeau

Allene Willson Groves
Marjorie Groves Mills

In addition, much credit is due County Librarians Carol Jaech and Terri Lehan and the magnificent staff at the Morgan Hill Library for providing constant and professional help; to former City Clerk Madge Soares for locating old records, to Larry Scettrini, a Historical Society researcher, who put a lot of things together for the first time; and to members of the Morgan Hill Historical Society Executive Boards from 1977-1985. But the work by Ralph Gonzales, my neighbor and friend, has been most directly valuable to me. Ralph is the one who painstakingly reproduced, sharpened, focused, and otherwise improved many of the photos that appear in the book. I also appreciate the assistance of the Fisher family in recent years, particularly that of Bob and Beverly Fisher and Betty Scheck Pinard.

Also, since the original publication, I have enjoyed the friendship and knowledge of Marjorie Groves Mills.

--Beth Dunham Wyman

FOR OLIVE

who scolded, corrected, cajoled,
encouraged, humored, promoted,
aided, edited, and finally approved.

Introduction

member of the Morgan Hill Historical Society once jokingly suggested adopting an organizational tee shirt with the emblem of El Toro mountain on the front and a caption beneath, reading "Ski Morgan Hill!" This play on words would probably have been no more confusing than the true fact of the matter. Most people quite logically assume that the distinctive peak overlooking the town is Morgan Hill, when actually it is El Toro Mountain, also known as Murphy's Peak.

To put things straight, the reader must understand that Hiram Morgan Hill was a man, not a mountain. He was a handsome Missourian who came to California in the 1870s to seek his fortune, decided to stay in San Francisco, became a bank employee and clothes model, and married Diana Helen Murphy, the daughter of the largest land-owner in the world. When Diana's father died she inherited 4,900 acres of the 8,927.10 acre Rancho Ojo de Agua de la Coche that is the City of Morgan Hill today. In 1886, after a long-postponed honeymoon in Europe, Morgan and Diana built a lovely country estate on this property and planned a happy future. For several years they enjoyed inviting friends from San Francisco and San Jose to visit and, since the home and ranch buildings were the only significant structures located between Madrone and San Martin, these guests would ask the train to stop at "Morgan Hill's." Thus, the place soon became known as "Morgan Hill," then later, as the Morganhill Station for the Southern Pacific railroad. The contracted version of the name was probably adopted in order to distinguish between the man and the place.

But fate intervened, causing the Hill's destiny to take a sharp turn. Because of a widely publicized lawsuit involving Morgan Hill's sister, the newly-weds did not settle on the ranch. Instead, they first escaped to Europe, then separated, with Morgan Hill establishing a headquarters at the Murphy ranch in Halleck, Nevada, and Diana and their daughter commuting between large homes in San Francisco and Washington, D.C. In 1892 the Morgan Hill ranch property was subdivided and sold in 10 to 100 acre parcels to settlers from as far away as South Dakota. Streets were laid out for a township, businesses were started, and the City of Morgan Hill, named for its first citizen and sub-divider, was incorporated on November 2, 1906.

Because so few are aware of this background and would be perfectly willing to "Ski Morgan Hill," and because so little information has been available about the man for whom the town was named, I became interested in the story of Hiram Morgan Hill. Because there were no known photographs of him I started a search that finally led to a distant relative who was still reluctant to talk after all these years because of the palimony scandal. But I got a photograph! I also visited the Northeastern Nevada Museum in Elko where period newspapers revealed the substance of Morgan Hill's last 30 years of life as a ranch owner and operator at Rancho Grande in Halleck and Devil's Gate northeast of Elko. During these years Morgan Hill was essentially separated from his wife and daughter and he became increasingly ill. He suffered a stroke in 1912 and died a year later in Elko. His remains were brought to the Santa Clara Catholic cemetery where he was laid to rest beside his father-in-law, Daniel Murphy.

Since Morgan Hill actually spent only a few short years in and around the town that was named for him it is not surprising he has been forgotten. I hope this book will restore the missing connection between the man and the town.

HIRAM
MORGAN HILL

Hiram Morgan Hill

iram Morgan Hill was born near Cape Girardeau, Missouri, on March 4, 1848. His Quaker father, Samuel Allen Hill, was a pioneer from Maryland, and his mother's family, the Sloans, had become wealthy from local lumber interests. Orphaned at an early age, Morgan and his younger sister, Sarah Althea, grew up in the Cape Girardeau home of their paternal grandparents located between Pacific and Independence Streets. They both received a comprehensive education at St. Vincent's Academy and probably would have lived out their lives in the Mississippi River town except for the fact that, at 22, Morgan reportedly fell in love with his first cousin. His guardian grandmother, who had children of her own to worry about, ordered him to leave the Cape immediately. So brother and sister departed for San Francisco where Morgan Hill became a bank employee. He also became a clothes

Reproduction of Morgan Hill's actual signature

Author's Photo

Hiram Morgan Hill
1848-1913

One of the few known photographs of Hiram Morgan Hill. The handsome sandy haired Missourian was more than six feet tall and he is shown here in 1881 at the age of 33, a year before he secretly married Diana Helen Murphy in San Francisco.

3

Author's Photos Courtesy Marjorie Groves Mills

Hiram Morgan Hill
*Photo taken in
San Francisco after 1870*

Hiram Morgan Hill
Photo dated April 25, 1871

model for the venerable haberdashery Bullock and Jones, which meant exposure at Palace Hotel fashion shows. A handsome and stylish bachelor who was always the picture of elegance, the tall, slender, blue eyed southerner drove a team of matched trotters and the finest buggy money could buy. So it's no surprise that in 1880 he caught the eye of Diana Helen Murphy. Since Diana's father was reported to be the "largest landowner in the world," she had no lack of suitors. But after meeting Morgan Hill she displayed no interest in anyone else.

However, Diana's father, Daniel, who had acquired millions of acres of land in several western states and Mexico, adamantly opposed a match. He felt that his beloved daughter could do better than a bank clerk and he disapproved of Hill's reputation as "fast." But, despite all efforts to discourage the couple, including a strategy by Diana's mother to arrange a betrothal between Diana and a distant cousin, Peter J. Colombet, the couple continued to meet. And in June of 1882, on a yacht in Santa Cruz harbor, Morgan Hill proposed marriage and Diana Murphy accepted.

DIANA HELEN MURPHY HILL

Diana Helen Murphy Hill

orn in 1859 at the Murphy family's San Martin ranch, Diana was a petite, spirited beauty who held high social ambitions. The daughter of Daniel Murphy and Maria Fisher, she had attended Murphy-founded Notre Dame College in San Jose. She was affectionately called "Dannie" by her father and "De-awhn" by everyone else. She was also known as the "Duchess of Durango" in reference to her father's millions of acres of Mexican landholdings.

When Diana was twenty-two she met thirty-three year old Hiram Morgan Hill, an heir to modest Missouri wealth and a cultured, well-educated southern gentleman. But there may have been some social distance. In addition to the eleven-year age difference there also was a disparity in lifestyles. Diana was part of a large, close-knit Irish Catholic family and Morgan, of Quaker extraction, had been orphaned at an early age. Then, too, there was no dispelling the insistent rumors about Morgan Hill's sister who had been dubbed "The Rose of Sharon" by the local press.

Diana Helen Murphy Hill
1859-1937

Diana (who insisted that her name be pronounced Dee-awhn) was small, about 5'2", and extremely beautiful with "eyes like violets." She inherited the passionate temperament of her pureblood Spanish grandmother, Liberata Ceseña Fisher Bull Piatti, and the fierce Irish determination of her father, Daniel Murphy, who was, at the time of his death, considered to be the largest landowner in the world.

Courtesy Bancroft Library

7

Diana Helen Murphy Hill
1859-1937

Diana Helen Murphy Hill was extremely ambitious even as a child, claiming to be a descendant of Irish kings and impatient with her rural San Martin surroundings. She embraced a lifelong pursuit of money and status which was finally fulfilled at age 63 when she married into English nobility.

Diana Helen Murphy

One of the few early photos of Diana. No date.

Nevertheless, love prevailed, and they were secretly married. The ceremony was performed by a discreet Methodist minister in San Francisco on July 31, 1882.

Two months later in Nevada, the bride's father, Daniel Murphy, was stricken with pneumonia after attempting to round up cattle in a blinding snowstorm. On his deathbed he called for his beloved "Dannie" and extracted a promise that she would never marry Morgan Hill.

Afterward, filled with remorse at her deception, Diana sought a divorce in Modesto on grounds that her father's dying wish haunted her. But friends and family successfully intervened, effecting a reconciliation, so that exactly a year after their wedding the young couple finally departed on a long-delayed honeymoon trip to Paris.

Diana Murphy Hill

An early photo of Diana Helen Murphy with her cousin, Amelia Fisher, in matching costumes.

Author's Photo
Courtesy Betty Pinard

Daniel Murphy

Youngest son of Martin Murphy Sr. and father of Diana Murphy who became Mrs. Morgan Hill. At the time of his death in 1882 Daniel was reportedly the "largest landowner in the world" with thousands of acres in California, Nevada and Mexico.

New York Weekly Graphic
November 22, 1887

San Jose Mercury News August 14, 1892   Courtesy Gilroy Historical Museum

Villa Miramonte

A sketch of Diana and Morgan Hill's Villa Miramonte in 1892 at the time of the Morgan Hill Ranch subdivision. This view is from the railroad tracks looking south toward El Toro Mountain, or Murphy's Peak.

In the meantime, after her father's death, Diana had inherited 4,900 acres of the original Rancho Ojo de Agua de la Coche, in the area that presently encompasses the City of Morgan Hill. By 1886 the newlyweds had established a country estate on the ranch property conveniently situated between Monterey Road and the railroad tracks. A turn-of-the-century home designed in the most fashionable Queen Anne style was surrounded by orchards and ranch buildings. It was fondly called Villa Miramonte. Tiffany-inspired stained glass windows adorned the front doors with the carved initials "MH" set inside roundels beneath. The hand-crafted brass doorknob was fashioned after the popular Gilbert and Sullivan operetta "The Mikado."

Detail of the hand-crafted brass doorknob of the Villa Miramonte probably inspired by the Gilbert and Sullivan operetta "The Mikado."

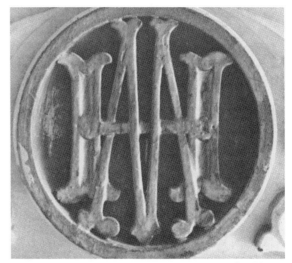

One of the two matching MH monograms that embellish the doors of the Villa Miramonte.

1978 Photo Courtesy Tim Kelly

The Villa Miramonte

A contemporary photo of the Villa Miramonte built by Morgan and Diana Hill on 4,900 acre portion of the Rancho Ojo de Agua de la Coche that Diana inherited after the death of her father. The home remains preserved in almost original condition, although it was damaged in both the 1984 Morgan Hill 6.1 earthquake and the 1989 Loma Prieta 7.1 earthquake.

The Villa Miramonte
Photo 1912-1913

Shows some of the original architectural detail and the thick wisteria that once decorated the porch. Photographer unknown.

12

DIANE MURPHY-HILL

Diane Murphy-Hill

organ and Diana Hill had only one child, Diane, born in 1884 two years after their marriage. This daughter was, of course, educated in the finest private schools at home and abroad, and pampered in a style appropriate to a fourth generation Murphy. When the Hills visited their country estate they would send a black coachman for Tina and Lucy Pinard of Madrone to play with little Diane. And when the Hills went to Europe to select furnishings for their home they brought back expensive gifts for the two local girls.

Diane was reported to be even more beautiful than her mother and, at twelve years old, she not only "resembled a French doll" but was fluent in three foreign languages. She spoke English to her father, Spanish to her mother and grandmother, French to the maid, and German to the cook. Her mother evidently transferred her own social ambitions onto Diane because it was well reported that Diana intended for her daughter to marry royalty or "at least a title." Diane, however, had her own opinion on the matter and firmly resisted all overtures with the argument that she "would rather marry an honest farmer."

Diane Murphy-Hill
1884-1912

The only child of Morgan and Diana Hill was educated in the best private schools at home and abroad.

15

Diane Murphy-Hill

At time of first communion June 11, 1896.

Diane Murphy-Hill
1884-1912

Shown here as a young woman who at twelve years, was reported to be more beautiful than her mother. She was fluent in three foreign languages.

After 1884 the Hills sought refuge from the incessant publicity about Morgan Hill's sister by first removing to Europe where they lived for more than eight years at #8 Avenue, Marceau, in Paris. After that, the family separated. Morgan Hill assumed the responsibility for the Murphy ranches in Nevada where he established a headquarters at Rancho Grande in Halleck while Diana and Diane alternated between residences in San Francisco and Washington D.C. In Washington, Diana remodeled the former British Legation building on Connecticut Avenue to suit her particular taste in living quarters and she hobnobbed with President Teddy Roosevelt and his "western" crowd.

In 1902 Diane made a formal debut in Washington society as "Miss Diane Murphy-Hill" after which she spent several years in Europe. There is no record of protracted activity during this period -- no course of study or suitable employment. It is most likely that, at her mother's insistence, Diane spent most of her time searching for a proper husband, willingly or not.

Miss Diane Murphy Hill
A Washington Debutante

The daughter of Diana and Morgan Hill shown at the time of her Washington D.C. debut in 1902. She firmly resisted her mother's social aspirations with the argument that she would "rather marry an honest farmer!"

Finally, when she was twenty-seven years old she married Hardouin de Reinach-Werth, a young French Baron who had been sent to Canada to supervise some family ranches. Thus, Diane became the Baroness Diane Murphy-Hill de Reinach-Werth, surely a title of enough hyphenated prestige to satisfy even her socially ambitious mother!

Four days after the wedding the father of the bride wrote that:

"Diane is now on the ocean with her husband, a charming, refined young man. They have been in love for five years and engaged to marry for three years. They ought to be very happy as all their tastes are alike. Diane has spent more than half her life in Europe."

Diane Murphy Hill

Photo probably taken in 1902 at the time of Washington D.C. debut at age 18.

Baron Hardouin de Reinach-Werth

The handsome, dark-complexioned Frenchman became the husband of Diane Murphy-Hill. He was 33 years old at the time of their marriage.

Diane Murphy-Hill de Reinach-Werth

A newspaper photo of 27-year-old Diane Murphy-Hill de Reinach-Werth at the time of her wedding on December 6, 1911 at St. Matthew's Cathedral in Washington, D.C.

Photos from Washington Post newspaper
December 7, 1911

The wedding ceremony was performed by an assistant pastor on December 6, 1911 at St. Matthew's Cathedral in Washington. One would have expected a crowd of well-dressed Murphys, perhaps the President and his friends, and an elegant reception. But, instead, the bride's parents, Mr. and Mrs. Morgan Hill, were the only witnesses. The following account appeared in the Washington Post the next day:

St. Matthews Cathedral Washington D.C.

A wedding of wide interest took place yesterday morning at St. Matthew's Church, when Miss Diane Morgan-Hill (sic), daughter of Mr. and Mrs. H. Morgan Hill, became the bride of Baron Hardouin de Reinach-Werth of France. The ceremony was performed at 11 o'clock by the Reverend Edward Ruckey, assistant pastor of St. Matthew's, and was witnessed only by the parents of the bride.

The bride wore the costume in which she later left Washington, a suit of navy blue whipcord with a large black hat trimmed with a white bow. She carried a small bouquet of lilies of the valley. Baron de Reinach-Werth and his bride took luncheon with Mr. and Mrs. Hill at their residence at 1230 Connecticut Avenue before leaving for New York whence they will sail this morning on the Loraine to spend two months in France. Upon their return to this country they will spend a month with Mr. and Mrs. Hill in Washington and will then go to Alberta, Canada, where Baron de Reinach-Werth has a ranch.

There is no report on the success of the honeymoon tour. However, a change of plans did occur. The young couple remained abroad until May -- several months longer than the two months projected by the newspaper account -- and, while still in Paris, Diane received news of her father's stroke at Devil's Gate ranch. She was expected to join him in June in Elko where he was recovering. But tragedy intervened and the lovely bride never returned. Instead, she suffered a nervous break-down, was hospitalized at St. Pancras sanitarium in London, and, on June 21st while her nurse's back was turned for a moment, she threw herself from a second story window onto cobblestones below. She was instantly killed from a massive skull fracture.

Contributing factors to this story include the rumor that the bridegroom had a drinking problem and had been sent to Canada for rehabilitation. Then, too, in those days when mental illness was poorly understood, there was a whisper about a "streak of insanity" that ran in the Hill family. The whispers probably gained legitimacy since Morgan Hill's sister was confined to the Stockton State Hospital for the last forty-five years of her life, and it was reported that Morgan Hill himself had "mentally deteriorated" before his death in Elko.

Diana went to London to make final arrangements for her daughter's burial and she brought the Baron back to Elko to help her with business affairs because, by then, Morgan Hill was recovering from a stroke and his condition was deteriorating. Diana brought a maid from her Washington home and rented a house in Elko where, with her son-in-law's assistance, she expected to nurse her husband back to health. Prior to his stroke, Morgan Hill's health had become steadily worse. He had become deaf, was reduced to using a cane, and had adopted a cavalier attitude toward his dress. In his last years in Nevada the once elegant clothes model is remembered wearing old bib overalls, a faded work shirt, and a slouch hat. In fact, Morgan Hill wrote this letter to his cousin Jennie Wilson in Cape Girardeau in December 1911:

"I am now in my 64th year, my wife is 50: but looks and feels 40. Very fond of society, bridge and visits with friends, and worships her family. I am totally deaf and have been so for the last three years. At one time I could hear with a Hutchinson Accoustican, but not a sound now.

I am still engaged in the ranching business in Nevada. I raise horses and cattle, I do not farm. I have been 30 years in this business. I love the free life, the open air. I am located 6500 feet above the sea, and at the ranch it is 15 below zero today. I go out in ten days to remain until next October. My wife has been on the ranch only once in her life. Diane was never there. They both greatly oppose what I do. But I could not lead an idle club life."

Unfortunately, he never recovered from the stroke in May and on November 13, 1913 he died from pneumonia "terminal to paresis" (paralysis). This was a little more than a year after his only daughter's suicide. He was nearly 66 years old. The occupation listed on the death certificate was "Stock Raiser." Almost half of his life had been spent on cattle ranches in Nevada. His son-in-law, "H.R. Werth," signed the final documents. His remains were sent to the Santa Clara Catholic cemetery for final disposition where he was laid to rest beside Daniel Murphy, the father-in-law who didn't approve!

Page 1

Metropolitan Club
Washington, D.C.

Dec 10, 1911

Dear Jennie,

You, Julia and I, being blood Cousins, and only a few of us, I have often thought, how strange that we saw, or heard so little of each other, I do not blame myself, for the feeling that existed between us as

Page 2

children has always remained with me.

I am now in my 64th year, my wife is 50: but looks and feels 40. Very fond of society; bridge whist friends, and worships her family. I am totally deaf, and have been so for the last three years. At one time, I could hear with a Hutchinson Acoustican, but not a sound now.

Page 3

I am still engaged in the ranching business in Nevada, I have horses and Cattle, I do not farm. I have been 30 years in this business, I love the free life, the open air. I am located 6500 ft above the Sea, and at the ranch it is 15 below Zero today, I go out in ten days to remain until next October. My wife has been

Page 4

on the ranch only once in her life. Diana who never there; they both greatly oppose what I do; but I could not lead an idle Club life.

Diana is now on the Ocean with her husband, a charming, refined young man. He is 30, she is 26: been in love 5 years and engaged 3 years. They ought to be very happy, as all their tastes are alike, Diana has spent more than half of her life in Europe. Tell my little Cousin that poor "Tagg" is dead. With love to you all

Morgan

Author's letters Courtesy Marjorie Groves Mills

23

No. **55345** *Application for License.*

DISTINCT OF COLUMBIA, ss:

Baron Hardouin de Reinach-Werth applicant for the issuance of a Marriage License to

the persons named herein, do solemnly swear (affirm) that the answers to the following interrogatories are true, to

the best of my knowledge and belief: So HELP ME GOD.

	MALE.	FEMALE.
Names	*Baron H. de Reinach-Werth*	*Diane Morgan Hill*
Ages	*33* years	*27* years
Color	*White*	*White*
Relationship	*None*	*None*
Former Marriages	*None*	*None*

Witness:

B'n H. de Reinach Werth

Subscribed and sworn to before me, this *1st* day of *Dec*, 191*1*

John E. Curry, Clerk.

By *N. A. Kuder*, Assistant Clerk.

No. **55345** **Marriage License.**

Reverend Edward L. Buckey authorized to celebrate marriages in the District of

Columbia, GREETING:

You are hereby authorized to celebrate the rites of marriage, between

Baron H. de Reinach-Werth, of *Alberta, Canada*

AND

Diane Morgan-Hill of *Wash., D.C.*

and having done so, you are commanded to make return of the same to the Clerk's Office of the Supreme Court

of the said District within TEN days, under a penalty of fifty dollars for default therein.

Witness my hand and seal of said Court, this *1st*

day of *Dec*, anno Domini 191*1*

, Clerk.

By *N A Kuder*, Assistant Clerk.

Application for marriage license by Diane Murphy-Hill and Hardouin de Reinach-Werth, December 1, 1911 Washington, D.C.

24

Saint Matthew's Cathedral
Washington, D. C.

Certificate of Marriage

The Records of this Cathedral Certify

that _Baron H. De Reinach-Werth_ and
Diane Morgan Hill

Were Lawfully Married

the _6th_ day of _December_ 19 _11_

In accordance with the Form of the Roman Catholic Church and the laws of this Republic.

Rev. _Edward L. Buchy_ Officiating

in the presence of

Diana M. Hill

and

Hiram Morgan Hill

Witnesses

Dated _____ Vol. ___ Pg. _____

Monsignor John J. Kuhn Rector
Assistant

Marriage Certificate of Diane Murphy-Hill and Baron Hardouin de Reinach-Werth

GIVEN AT THE GENERAL REGISTER OFFICE, LONDON

Application Number CAS 307909/83

	REGISTRATION DISTRICT *St. Pancras*								

1912 DEATH in the Sub-district of *West St. Pancras* in the *County of London*

Columns:— 1	2	3	4	5	6	7	8	9
No.	When and Where died	Name and surname	Sex	Age	Occupation	Cause of death	Signature, description and residence of informant	When registered	Signature of registrar
153	21st June 1912 9 Saint George's Terrace Saint Pancras	Diane de Reinach Werth	Female	27 years	Wife of Hardwin de Reinach Werth a farmer near Calgary Alberta Canada	Compression of Brain fracture of skull Fell into area when she jumped from window to kill herself temporary insanity	Certificate received from H. Schröder Coroner for London Inquest held 24th June 1912	Twenty fifth June 1912	Thomas P. Parkin Registrar.

CERTIFIED to be a true copy of an entry in the certified copy of a Register of Deaths in the District above mentioned.
Given at the GENERAL REGISTER OFFICE, LONDON, under the Seal of the said Office, the *17th* day of *August* 1983

DX 286280

Form A504M Dd 8264467 20м 8/82 Mcr(300023)

Death Certificate of Diane de Reinach-Werth

Nevada State Board of Health

BUREAU OF VITAL STATISTICS

STANDARD DEATH CERTIFICATE

1. PLACE OF DEATH

County of *Elko*

Town of *Elko*

or

City of .... (No. .... St.; .... Ward)

State Index No. ....

Local Registered No. *6 2*

[If death occurred in a hospital or institution, give its NAME instead of street and number, and fill out No. 18.]

2. FULL NAME *Hiram Morgan Hill*

PERSONAL AND STATISTICAL PARTICULARS	MEDICAL CERTIFICATE OF DEATH

3. SEX *Male*

4. COLOR OR RACE *White*

5. Single, Married, Widowed, or Divorced (Write the word.) *Married*

6. DATE OF BIRTH *March 4 848* (Month) (Day) (Year)

7. AGE *65* years, *8* months, *19* days. If LESS than 1 day, ... hrs., or .... min.

8. OCCUPATION (a) Trade, profession, or particular kind of work *Stock Raiser* (b) General nature of industry, business, or establishment in which employed (or employer)

9. BIRTHPLACE (State or country) *Mo*

PARENTS

10. NAME OF FATHER *Samuel Allen Hill*

11. BIRTHPLACE OF FATHER (State or country) *Maryland*

12. MAIDEN NAME OF MOTHER *Julia Ann Sloan*

13. BIRTHPLACE OF MOTHER (State or country) *Mo*

13a. LENGTH OF RESIDENCE

At place of death *2* years, *—* months

In Nevada *31* years, *—* months

14. The above is true to the best of my knowledge.

(Informant) *H. R. Werth*

(Address) *Elko Nev.*

15. Filed ...., 191..

Filed *Nov 27*, 191*3* *John E. Worden*

Subregistrar

Registrar or Deputy

16. DATE OF DEATH *November 23rd*, 191*3* (Month) (Day) (Year)

17. I HEREBY CERTIFY that I attended deceased from *May 19th*, 1912, to *Nov 23rd*, 191*3*

that I last saw h *im* alive on *Nov 23rd*, 191*3*

and that death occurred, on the date stated above, at *7.15 P.* m.

The CAUSE OF DEATH* was as follows:

Lobar Pneumonia

terminal to General paresis

.... (Duration) *1* yrs., *6* mos., ... ds.

Contributory .... (Secondary)

.... (Duration) .... yrs., ... mos., ... ds.

(Signed) *C W West* M.D.

Nov 25th, 191*3* (Address) *Elko Nevada*

*State the DISEASE CAUSING DEATH, or, in deaths from VIOLENT CAUSES, state (1) MEANS OF INJURY; and (2) whether ACCIDENTAL, SUICIDAL, or HOMICIDAL.

18. SPECIAL INFORMATION only for Hospitals, Institutions, Transients, or Recent Residents.

Former or usual residence .... How long at place of death .... days

Where was disease contracted, if not at place of death?

19. PLACE OF BURIAL OR REMOVAL *Santa Clara Calif*

DATE OF BURIAL *Nov 27th*, 191*3*

20. UNDERTAKER *J. L. Keyser*

ADDRESS *Elko Nev,*

Death Certificate of Hiram Morgan Hill

Gravestone of Hiram Morgan Hill in Santa Clara Catholic Cemetery

Courtesy Joyce Hunter

27

The Elko Miramonte

A 1914 view of the grand living room in the Elko, Nevada home built by Diana Murphy-Hill. Family photos and collections adorn the walls and tables. Diana often entertained with lavish gourmet dinners, dansants, and Sunday afternoon teas in this imposing home set high on a hill overlooking the town.

Courtesy Tom Clark

The Elko Miramonte 1983

A photo of the grand living room as it appeared in 1983.
(Compare to 1914 photo page 28.)

Before her husband died, Diana, now 53 years old, had plans drawn for a new Villa Miramonte in Elko. At the same time, for reasons never disclosed, the Hills legally adopted their son-in-law. The lavish 10,000 square foot house was constructed with separate living quarters for each member of the family and for the servants, but with large common areas as well. It was a very imposing structure -- two stories with a full basement and a detached carriage house -- set in solitary splendor atop a high hill overlooking the town. Once again, as in Morgan Hill, the latest architectural design was followed. This time it was a Frank Lloyd Wright inspired Prairie style house with some old fashioned bungalow gables.

After Morgan Hill's death the Baron (now an adopted son) continued to reside with Diana in Elko where he became well known and highly regarded. He drove a fashionable red Stutz Bearcat automobile and often accompanied local men on hunting trips. He introduced pig raising as an innovation at the ranches and he shipped horses to France. In Elko he is fondly remembered as a "man's man."

Diana frequently entertained, always with the Baron at her side -- he was called Captain Werth in Elko --a lifestyle considered quite bold by the local townspeople. However, this period came to an abrupt end when World War I began in 1914. The Captain was called to French military service. He fought for his country during the war, later married a French actress, and was, apparently, lost forever to his American friends and relatives.

The Elko Miramonte 1983

A photo of the exterior of the Prairie-Bungalow style home built by Diana Murphy-Hill in Elko. Looking from Court Street toward the original formal entrance steps.

In Elko it was believed that Diana missed the Captain keenly. After he left she lavished her attentions on some purebred Pomeranians and continued to entertain frequently. She remained in Elko until 1917 when she sold Rancho Grande and Devil's Gate. She kept only part of the Haystack ranch northwest of Elko. In 1919 she sold the Elko Miramonte and in 1922 she went to London where she finally achieved her coveted title. At 63 she married Sir George Rhodes, a cousin of British Empire builder Cecil Rhodes, who endowed the famous Rhodes Scholarships and for whom

Rhodesia was named. Becoming Lady Rhodes suited Diana very well and she was at last content, but the reverie did not last long. George Rhodes died in 1924 at their villa on the Riviera and after that, Diana was often seen at the gambling tables of Monte Carlo where she occasionally paid off enormous debts with her remaining California and Nevada properties. She contracted tuberculosis and died in Cannes on December 17, 1937 at the age of 78.

It was the same year that marked the death of her sister-in-law, Sarah Althea Hill.

30

Lady Diana Rhodes
1859-1937

The still beautiful Diana Murphy Hill in 1922 at the age of 63 as she appeared at her presentation before King George V of England.

SARAH ALTHEA HILL

Sarah Althea Hill

n Valentine's Day in 1937 an old woman with white hair and a lame hip died from influenza at the Stockton State Hospital -- formerly called the Stockton Insane Asylum. Her death certificate also noted that she had suffered from dementia praecox (schizophrenia) for "years." This woman, once beautiful and courageous, was the sister of Morgan Hill who fought a public battle for palimony at the time when even divorce was not socially condoned. The concept of palimony was unheard of. But although the legal skirmishes had been spirited with almost equal wins and losses, the fight had taken its toll. And, as a hospital patient, Sarah insisted on being treated as the grand and wealthy lady she once hoped to become. She often held court on the grounds, and her delusions, if they were such, could not be lightly dismissed, because the truth was even more incredible.

Courtesy Bancroft Library

Sarah Althea Hill Sharon Terry
1857-1937

Morgan Hill's sister, shown here in her early thirties during the more than six year litigation with Senator William Sharon of San Francisco and Nevada. She is wearing a special gold bracelet given to her by her husband, attorney David S. Terry, whom she married after Sharon died.

35

Sarah Althea Hill

San Francisco photo dated August 25, 1871 when "Allie" was 18 years old.

**Hiram Morgan Hill
and
Sarah Althea Hill**

The only known photograph of Hiram Morgan Hill and his sister Sarah Althea Hill. San Francisco photo dated August 25, 1871 when Morgan Hill was 23 years old and Sarah Althea was 18.

Sarah Althea Hill was born near Cape Girardeau, Missouri in 1857, orphaned as a young child, and reared by affluent grandparents at the Cape where she and her brother attended a private school, St. Vincent's Academy. In 1870 Sarah joined Morgan in San Francisco, living with relatives for a time and quickly disposing of her $20,000 inheritance. In 1880 she was recovering from a broken engagement to a young San Francisco attorney, Reuben Lloyd, that ended dramatically, when she attempted to swallow a lethal dose of laudanum in Lloyd's office. Fortunately, she was saved by a prompt call for treatment. The ex-fiance was a partner of the son-in-law of former Nevada Senator William Sharon. So, given Sharon's libertine reputation with women, it was no surprise that soon after the laudanum incident the 60-year-old widower invited the 23-year-old Missouri beauty to his office to "discuss investments."

Sharon was fabulously wealthy as a result of fortunate Nevada silver mine stock investments and manipulations, and he was known as "King of the Comstock Lode." After the untimely and improbable death of his partner, William Ralston, Sharon fell into the ownership of numerous large properties in Nevada and in California including the Palace and Grand Hotels in San Francisco and the Ralston Estate in Belmont.

Overcome by her beauty at his meeting with Sarah Althea, Sharon quickly proposed a deal. He offered to pay her $1,000 a month if she would become his mistress. Sarah was deeply offended and left his office. But soon after, Sharon proposed a second offer that was more agreeable. He offered to pay her $500 a month if she would live with him, and, to satisfy Sarah's need for propriety in the matter, he agreed to sign a marriage contract affirming their relationship, but on the condition that the document be kept a secret for two years.

Sarah was soon installed in rooms at the Grand Hotel which was connected by a second story "bridge of sighs" to the Palace Hotel where the Senator lived. The marriage contract was signed on August 25, 1880 and the relationship flourished for fifteen months. Then Sarah discovered that her paramour was unfaithful. She charged him with adultery and named nine women. She offered the marriage contract as proof of their married status. She also demanded recompense.

The Senator, outraged at her audacity, ordered the hinges removed from her door and the carpets taken up. He also filed suit in federal Circuit Court to have the alleged marriage contract declared a fraud. A month later, Sarah Althea countered with a suit in Superior Court charging desertion, adultery, and demanding alimony and proper division of property. She estimated her share to be in the neighborhood of $10 million. Sharon's case was called *Sharon vs. Hill* while Sarah Althea's was called *Sharon vs. Sharon*. Claims and counterclaims relating to these two cases continued for more than six

Courtesy Bancroft Library

Sarah Althea Hill Sharon
1857-1937

The "stunningly beautiful" Sarah made headlines with every court appearance during the simultaneous litigation of Sharon vs. Sharon and Sharon vs. Hill because she seemed to have endless costumes and because she reportedly carried a pearl-handled revolver in her purse.

William Sharon
1819-1885

The former U.S. Senator from Nevada who allegedly signed a secret marriage contract with Sarah Althea Hill when he was 60 and she was 23. He was known as "King of the Comstock Lode."

years with every one of the numerous court appearances making headlines because Sarah was not only "stunningly beautiful" -- described by an admiring judge as "a golden-haired beauty with sparkling blue eyes" -- but she was full of brass and bounce and loved to shoot guns and make a lot of noise. Everyone agreed that she was vivacious and quick-witted and headstrong. It was rumored that she fingered a pearl-handled revolver in her handbag as she listened to the often scandalous testimony by Sharon's witnesses she accused of being "paid" and she once announced that she could "hit a four bit piece nine times out of ten." She swore she would "shoot" one of the witnesses because of his "lies."

The two cases ran concurrently to the delight of the local newspapers for whom the testimony provided a bonanza. They were quick to dub Sarah Althea the "Rose of Sharon." But the divorce case

**Text of the Marriage Contract
between Sarah Althea Hill and Senator William Sharon
August 25, 1880**

In the City and County of San Francisco, State of California, on the 25th day of August, A.D. 1880, I, Sarah Althea Hill, of the City and County of San Francisco, State of California, age 27 years, do here in the presence of Almighty God, take Senator William Sharon, of the State of Nevada, to be my lawful wedded husband, and do here acknowledge and declare myself to be the wife of Senator William Sharon of the State of Nevada.

**Sarah Althea Hill
August 25th, 1880, San Francisco, Cal.**

I agree not to make known the contents of this paper and its existence for two years unless Mr. Sharon himself sees fit to make it known.

S.A. Hill

In the City and County of San Francisco, State of California, on the 25th day of August, A.D. 1880, I, Senator William Sharon, of the State of Nevada, age 60 years, do here, in the presence of Almighty God, take Sarah Althea Hill, of the City of San Francisco, Cal., to be my lawful and wedded wife, and do here acknowledge myself to be the husband of Sarah Althea Hill.

**Wm. Sharon, Nevada
August 25, 1880**

Sarah Althea's death certificate contradicts the age given in the marriage contract. It is possible that Sarah added four years to her age in order to appear older than her 23 years.

was settled after fifteen months when the Superior Court ruled *in favor* of Sarah Althea. The marriage contract, the court declared, was valid. She had been legally married and could be legally divorced. On February 16, 1885, Sarah Althea was awarded $2500 a month alimony and $60,000 for counsel's fees even though Senator Sharon insisted on the witness stand that he had made a "settlement in full" in the amount of $7,500 when his relationship with "Allie" was terminated in November of 1881. Sarah did not contest this, but claimed he had defaulted on his final three payments.

With the announcement that she was legally "Mrs. Sharon," Sarah Althea threw a party for 200 and went on a shopping spree. In addition, the soon-to-be wealthy divorcee began appearing in daily changes of costume. Endless newspaper copy was devoted to descriptions of Sarah Althea's apparel which was ordered directly from Paris and unlike anything San Francisco had ever seen. Her dresses were made of serpent-green brocade and lemon silk, styled with poufs, and decorated with pearl embroidery and passementerie. She wore custom designed sealskin and astrachan jackets while ostrich-tip pom-poms decorated her high-piled coif-

fure. On the thirty-third day of the marriage contract trial she appeared in a dress of brocaded velvet half concealed by the unbuttoned length of a tailor-made coat. But high-style was not enough to deter the legal process.

Sharon's attorneys immediately filed for a new trial and this was set eight months later, on November 13. Unfortunately, the 65 year old defendant, Senator Sharon, died on that very day so the hearing was carried over. A month later the other court handed down a decision in the "marriage contract" case. First they declared that Circuit Court held jurisdiction over Superior Court in the matter because their case had been filed first. Second, they ruled that the alleged marriage contract as well as the numerous "Dear Wife" letters introduced as evidence by the defense were false and forged. Sarah Althea was ordered to deliver the document for cancellation.

So at the end of 1885, after two full years of litigation, Sarah Althea's legal status was this:

- Her husband was dead
- She was legally a widow
- She had a Superior Court ruling in *Sharon vs. Sharon* upholding the 1880 marriage contract and awarding her a divorce, alimony, and counsel fees.

She also had a federal Circuit Court decision in *Sharon vs. Hill* declaring the marriage contract a fraud and demanding that the document be relinquished and cancelled.

To date she had received no compensation at all and at least $5,000 of her court expenses had been borne by an old Missouri acquaintance, Mary Ellen Pleasant. Mary Ellen was a black woman known as "Mammy Pleasant" who operated boarding houses and other businesses in San Francisco. It was believed that she had money, influence, and voodoo powers. She appeared to be a faithful friend and staunch supporter of Sarah Althea's cause. But there was another strong supporter, too. He was Sarah Althea's associate defense attorney, former Justice of the Supreme Court, David Smith Terry, who had been recently widowed and who had become fiercely protective of his client during the lengthy litigation.

Terry was a Kentucky gunfighter who probably admired Sarah's spirit. More important, he was known to be an unrelenting foe of the moneyed interests in California, a group to which Senator Sharon most certainly belonged. Terry had been replaced on the Supreme Court bench by the very same Justice Stephen Field who was now presiding over the marriage contract case in Circuit Court. And, perhaps more to the point, he fought and won a duel with U.S. Senator David Broderick over an 1858 election insult. In other words, Terry wasn't one to let things slide! He was a 6'3" giant of a man who customarily carried a bowie knife under his jacket and in 1885 he was a lonely widower who had personally taken on Sarah Althea's cause celebre. Twelve days after the adverse Circuit Court ruling against Sarah Althea the two became man and wife. He was 61. She was 28. Undeniably, the southern belle had a way with older men!

David Smith Terry
1823-1889

The Kentucky gunfighter who became an associate defense attorney for Sarah Althea Hill Sharon in Sharon vs. Sharon and married his client after Sharon died. He was 61 and she was 28. There is no denying the fact that Sarah had a way with older men.

Sarah Althea Sharon Terry
1857-1937

Sarah Althea shown here in one of her many elegant costumes.

Sarah Althea Hill and William Sharon

David S. Terry and Mammy Pleasant

Sketched during the trial by an artist for Alta California, June 1, 1884

As an attorney and former Supreme Court justice, Terry must have had some legal doubt about his wife's case against Sharon. But litigation of this type is like war. After a time the reason for fighting becomes less important than the fighting itself. Too, Terry probably felt that Sarah was placed at a great disadvantage to Sharon's money and influence. Thus, the more she was attacked, the more passionately he defended. "I will not have my wife made out to be a strumpet," he declared.

The next legal move occurred in Superior Court when Sharon's son and heir asked for a new trial in the divorce case. This was denied and immediately appealed. But the State Supreme Court upheld Sarah's marriage contract and the award for alimony and fees. This was October 1886 and three long years had passed. However, disposition of the appeal did not occur until a year later when, with a new court in session, the marriage contract decision was again affirmed but the amount of alimony was reduced from $2500 a month to $500 a month. Counsel fees were disallowed. Sarah Althea had yet to see a cent!

The next move was also made by Sharon's side to compel the surrender of the marriage contract for cancellation. This bill of revivor was initiated even though the time for appeal had expired. It named David S. Terry as an additional defendant. The Terrys demurred and the case was argued before a panel of judges who announced that the final decision would be handed down on September 3, 1888.

However, before that date arrived, one of the judges was returning by train from Los Angeles to San Francisco. The Terrys lived midway at Terry's ranch in Fresno and coincidentally boarded the same San Francisco bound train. As they walked through the judge's car Sarah Althea tweaked his hair and, was reported to have glared at him "viciously." She also spoke loudly, within his hearing, of the desirability of drowning certain individuals in the bay. The good judge was understandably upset and warned the San Francisco court to have sufficient deputies on hand for the September 3 hearing in order to prevent a disturbance.

The Sharon cases had attracted immense notoriety so the courtroom and corridors were crowded when the Circuit Court finally met to announce the long-awaited decision. Three federal judges were joined by a district judge. The Terrys were seated before them at the trial table and Sarah Althea held a small satchel which, it was later revealed, contained a loaded .45 calibre Colt's pistol. The opinion was read by Justice Field. He dryly reviewed the evidence then restated the entire case. He again condemned the unvirtuous conduct of the

defendant, Sarah Althea, without mentioning Sharon's admitted participation; and it was necessary to execute some fancy legal footwork to justify the conclusion that federal court held jurisdiction in the matter and that the appeal period was valid. The court record of this reading covers 30 pages.

To most observers it was clear very early on what the decision would be. One can imagine Terry's temper rising. Finally, after Judge Field had been reading for a long period of time, Sarah Althea stood up and startled the court room by shouting, "Justice Field, I hear you have been paid!" She was releasing the catch on her satchel when Field ordered her to sit down. Then, as her tirade gathered force, he ordered her removed from the courtroom. Terry moved to his wife's side immediately and attempted to quiet her, but when the marshal started to take her away Terry hit him so hard he broke his tooth. Terry was then overpowered by deputies and pinned to the floor. Sarah's satchel was snatched away and she was dragged kicking and screaming, from the room. The deputies let Terry get up to follow but, by this time, the corridor was clogged with spectators so Terry was forced to pull a nine-inch bowie knife to clear the way. The deputies swarmed over him again. One held him at pistol point while the other, David Naegle, removed the knife from his hand.

When some order had been restored the court went back to its opinion and Justice Field read on, seemingly unperturbed, for another hour! The judges then retired for fifteen minutes, after which they solemnly filed back to the courtroom where they announced that the Terrys were guilty of contempt of court. Terry was given six months in Alameda County jail. Sarah was given thirty days.

After this the legal proceedings grew furious. Terry filed several appeals from his jail cell, all of which were denied. He also threatened to "kill" Justice Field. Because of this and other threats, and because of the excessive passion invested in the two cases, Justice Field was given a special deputy for his personal protection. The guard was David Naegle, the federal marshal who had taken the knife from Terry in the courtroom. Naegle was a former police chief from Tombstone, Arizona, who had killed two men. So Terry's threats, modified from "killing" to a promise that he would "slap Justice Field's face or horsewhip him if he had the opportunity," didn't scare Naegle. He was prepared for the worst.

Almost a year later, on the 14th of August in 1889, the "opportunity" presented itself in a Lathrop railroad station restaurant when Justice Field and Naegle noticed Sarah Althea and Terry enter the room where they were dining. Sarah turned abruptly and withdrew, presumably to arm herself, but her husband walked straight to the

Sarah Althea Terry

Newspaper sketch from The San Francisco Chronicle, August 15, 1889.

Ex-Judge David Smith Terry

Deputy David Naegle

Justice Stephen Field

72-year-old Justice Field and slapped his face twice. Before he could slap him again, Naegle, still sitting, shot Terry dead. Screaming, Sarah returned to the room and cradled her husband's bleeding body in her arms. Finally, she was led away in a daze. Field and Naegle were both arrested for murder but Field, who had influence with the Governor of California, managed to have his charges transferred to San Francisco where they were dropped. Naegle was tried and found innocent. He was successful in the defense that he had acted "only in the course of duty," a precept still in effect today. In fact, Naegle's case set a precedent that a federal officer cannot be prosecuted in a state court for acts done in the performance of his duty.

The Shooting of Judge Terry in the Lathrop Restaurant

From Wagstaff's Life of David S. Terry

Terry was buried on a simmering hot day at St. John's Church in Stockton. Sarah tried to arrange a proper Catholic burial but was unsuccessful. She was also turned down by the Mexican Veterans and the California Pioneers, both groups to which Terry unquestionably belonged. Evidently the stream of publicity surrounding the event of Terry's death inspired caution in everyone. Even a clergyman could not be found to read the funeral service so a layman performed that duty. The honorary pallbearer included longtime associates of the former Judge. Sarah was attended by her brother, Morgan Hill, and Frank Rodney, a cousin. Persons of any prominence were notably absent. But a curious crowd packed the church despite the intense valley heat, and all eyes were on Sarah when, during the reading of the First Epistle to St. Paul, her body weaved back and forth. Then she rose unsteadily to lean upon the coffin, and during the final prayer she bowed her head and sobbed aloud. As the final words were spoken, Sarah gazed long and earnestly at the face of her beloved. "Oh, my darling," she murmured. "You were shot down without a moment's warning." After that she asked, to herself, "Is this the last?" Then, turning toward the crowd, she repeated in a louder voice, "Is this the last?"

48

Taking the body from the morgue.

Pallbearers taking body into St. John's Church. Terry's comrade, General Camaran, of the Mexican War, standing by hearse door.

Sketches from the *San Francisco Chronicle* August 17, 1889
"The Funeral of Judge Terry at Stockton"

Sarah's brother and cousin accompanied her to the Hotel Yosemite for a few days of recuperation where they kept the widow in seclusion from the hounding press. Then Sarah returned to her Fresno home for what should have been a period of peace and quiet. However, Sarah seemed in no mood to relax or admit defeat. She was despondent one day, planning bitter revenge the next. She quarreled with the executor of Terry's estate over money; she attempted to file an appeal for her share of Sharon's millions; her interest in extrasensory perception was revived and she believed herself in communication with her dead husband. She even reported being robbed of valuables but police concluded it had been a hallucination. During this period a reporter wrote that Sarah Althea had been through "more sensational experiences in...about eight years than any other woman alive." Sarah's changed appearance was cause for alarm, too. At only 35 her face was lined, her hair disheveled and streaked with gray, and she displayed absolutely no interest in visitors. In February of 1892 the San Francisco Chronicle reported that "the long mental strain to which Sarah had been subjected and the defeat of her hopes and ambitions...have had the inevitable result." Shortly thereafter, a San Francisco physician declared she was insane but described it as a mild and treatable case not requiring hospitalization. Sarah was returned to Mammy Pleasant's care where, for a time, it appeared she was recovering. There was talk of a lecture tour for which Mammy bought six trunks of new clothes for her charge. But soon the irrational behavior resumed. Sarah was observed standing in the rain, covered with mud, at the corner of Kearny and Post Streets. And when she was refused admittance to a second-rate Market Street hotel she attacked the clerk. Finally, after being found wandering in the streets, blank-eyed and dressed in a satin ball gown, Sarah Althea was locked up pending a sanity hearing. On the recommendation of her guardian, Mammy Pleasant, she was committed to the state asylum for the insane. On March 11, 1892 in the custody of a deputy sheriff, Sarah Althea Hill Sharon Terry, "The Rose of Sharon," was taken to Stockton where she remained for the next forty-five years.

Even though, for all intents and purposes, the two court cases were settled with the September 3 decision, the legal skirmishing continued on all fronts and, just six weeks before Terry's killing (and six years after the suit was filed!), the State Supreme Court, on an appeal by Sharon's heirs, unanimously reversed the first divorce case ruling. It held that "the parties (Sarah and the Senator) did not cohabit in the usual way of married people," therefore their relationship was merely one of "man and mistress" and not one of husband and wife.

This determination established the guiding principle in similar cases for 90 years until, in 1979, a Los Angeles court ruled in *Marvin vs. Marvin* that an unmarried couple who lived together could make a binding agreement, expressly or implied by their conduct, to share property or support one another after they parted. Although no such agreement was found in the Marvin case, the plaintiff, Michelle Triolta, who had lived with actor Lee Marvin for six years without benefit of matrimony, was awarded "equity" in the sum of $104,000. Since that time other so-called palimony cases have received similar judgments.

Although long forgotten, Sarah was buried in the Terry family plot in the rural cemetery at Stockton, after her February 14 death in 1937 at the state hospital.

STATE OF CALIFORNIA
DEPARTMENT OF PUBLIC HEALTH
VITAL STATISTICS

STANDARD CERTIFICATE OF DEATH

1. PLACE OF DEATH: DIST. NO. **3950**
COUNTY OF **San Joaquin**
CITY, TOWN OR RURAL DISTRICT OF **Stockton, Calif.**
LOCAL REGISTERED NO. **289**
STREET AND NO. **Stockton St te Hospital**
IF DEATH OCCURRED IN A HOSPITAL OR INSTITUTION, GIVE IT NAME INSTEAD OF STREET AND NO.

2. FULL NAME **Sarah A. Terry,**
RESIDENCE: NO. **Stockton State Hospital**
USUAL PLACE OF ABODE
IF NON RESIDENT, GIVE ST. CITY OR TOWN, AND STATE.

3. SEX **Female** 4. COLOR OR RACE **White** 5. SINGLE, MARRIED, WIDOWED OR DIVORCED? (WRITE THE WORD) **Widowed**

5A. IF MARRIED, WIDOWED OR DIVORCED, NAME OF HUSBAND OR WIFE **David S Terry**

6. DATE OF BIRTH **1857**
MONTH DAY YEAR

7. AGE **80** YR. MO. DAYS IF LESS THAN ONE DAY HRS. MIN.

OCCUPATION
8. TRADE, PROFESSION OR KIND OF WORK DONE AS SPINNER, SAWYER, BOOKKEEPER, ETC. **none**
9. INDUSTRY OR BUSINESS IN WHICH WORK WAS DONE, AS SILKMILL, SAWMILL, BANK, ETC.
10. DATE DECEASED LAST WORKED AT THIS OCCUPATION (MO. AND YR.)
11. TOTAL YEARS SPENT IN THIS OCCUPATION

12. BIRTHPLACE (CITY OR TOWN) **Unknown**
STATE OR COUNTRY **United States**

FATHER
13. NAME **Unknown**
14. BIRTHPLACE (CITY OR TOWN) **Unknown**
STATE OR COUNTRY **Unknown**

MOTHER
15. MAIDEN NAME **Unknown**
16. BIRTHPLACE (CITY OR TOWN) **Unknown**
STATE OR COUNTRY **Unknown**

17. LENGTH OF RESIDENCE
A. CITY, TOWN OR RURAL DISTRICT OF DEATH **44** YRS. **11** MOS. **3** DAYS **Unk**
B. IN CALIFORNIA YRS. MOS. DAYS
C. IN U.S., IF OF FOREIGN BIRTH **life** YRS. MOS. DAYS

18. INFORMANT (SIGNATURE) **Hospital Records,**
ADDRESS **Stockton State Hospital**

19. BURIAL, CREMATION OR REMOVAL (WRITE THE WORD) **Burial**
PLACE **Rural Cemetery Stockton, Calif.** DATE **2/19/37**
1528

20. EMBALMER LICENSE NO. **A. Virchaux**
SIGNATURE
FUNERAL DIRECTOR **DeYoung & Conklin**
ADDRESS **Stockton, Calif.**

21. FILED **Feb.16/37**
DAY LOCAL REGISTRAR **Deputy**

22. DATE OF DEATH **Feb. 14, 1937**
MONTH DAY YEAR

23. MEDICAL CERTIFICATE OF DEATH
I HEREBY CERTIFY, THAT I ATTENDED DECEASED FROM **Dec 1/31**
TO **Feb 14/37**
THAT I LAST SAW H. **er** ALIVE ON **Feb 14/37**
AND THAT DEATH OCCURRED ON THE ABOVE STATED DATE AT THE HOUR OF **1:00 a m**
THE PRINCIPAL CAUSE OF DEATH AND RELATED CAUSES OF IMPORTANCE, IN ORDER OF ONSET, WERE AS FOLLOWS: DATE OF ONSET
Influenza with pneumonia **Feb 10, 1937**
OTHER CONTRIBUTORY CAUSES OF IMPORTANCE: **Dementia Praecox** **years ago**
(11)
IF OPERATION, DATE OF WAS THERE AN AUTOPSY?
CONDITION FOR WHICH PERFORMED
NAME LABORATORY TEST CONFIRMING DIAGNOSIS

24. CORONER'S CERTIFICATE OF DEATH
I HEREBY CERTIFY, THAT I TOOK CHARGE OF THE REMAINS DESCRIBED ABOVE, HELD AN INQUEST, AUTOPSY OR INQUIRY THEREON, AND FROM SUCH ACTION FIND THAT SAID DECEASED CAME TO H. DEATH ON THE DATE STATED ABOVE.

25. IF DEATH WAS DUE TO EXTERNAL CAUSES (VIOLENCE) FILL IN THE FOLLOWING:
ACCIDENT, SUICIDE OR HOMICIDE? DATE OF INJURY
INJURED AT { CITY OR TOWN OF COUNTY AND STATE OF
DID INJURY OCCUR IN HOME, INDUSTRY, OR PUBLIC PLACE?
MANNER OF INJURY
NATURE OF INJURY

26. IF DISEASE/INJURY RELATED TO OCCUPATION, SPECIFY

27. SIGNATURE **Grace M Cosley** M.D.
PHYSICIAN AUTOPSY SURGEON
ADDRESS **Stockton State Hospital**

28. WHEN REQUIRED BY LAW CORONER
COUNTY OF

Death Certificate of Sarah Althea Hill Sharon Terry

51

MARY ELLEN
"MAMMY" PLEASANT

Mary Ellen "Mammy" Pleasant

uring the lengthy trials, a curious stream of witnesses appeared to render often bizarre and conflicting testimony. The two original cases spawned half a dozen other cases -- including the prosecution and conviction of one of Sarah Althea's witnesses for preparing a false affidavit and an attempt to remove Sharon's leading attorney from the bar on the grounds of perjury. But the strangest aspect, by far, of the *Sharon vs. Sharon* and *Sharon vs. Hill* litigation was the faithful attendance at each of the many hearings by Mary Ellen "Mammy" Pleasant, a black housekeeper for a local banker, Thomas Bell. Bell had been closely associated with Sharon's former Bank of California partner, William Ralston. Mammy Pleasant was reputed to have considerable means and important connections and her dedication to Sarah's cause bore out the theory that she must have had a financial interest in the outcome of the case. Each morning before court was in session she arrived in an elegant carriage drawn by a team of bay horses. Her place in the courtroom was immediately behind the Terrys where she could oc-

Mary Ellen "Mammy" Pleasant
1815-1904

A principal character in the Sharon vs. Hill and Sharon vs. Sharon litigation.

casionally confer with one or both defendants. Unlike Sarah who managed to appear in daily changes of costume, Mammy Pleasant always appeared in unrelieved black. She pulled the brim of a huge black straw hat tightly down around her face so that, in the words of the eager press, it resembled a coal scoop. On the witness stand she offered as little information as possible but she did admit to having known the plaintiff for "two years." Many, however, believed that the acquaintance had begun long before in Missouri when Mammy was in the employ of Sarah's Cape Girardeau family and Sarah was but a child. One of the judges wrote this revealing description:

> *Mary E. Pleasant, better known as Mammy Pleasant, is a conspicuous and important figure in this affair, without whom it would probably never have been brought before the public. She appears to be a shrewd old negress of considerable means, who has lived in San Francisco many years, and who is engaged in furnishing and fitting up houses and rooms, and caring for women and girls who need a manager or a mammie, as the case may be.*

Sarah Althea probably needed both, and in that regard, Mammy Pleasant did own up to the fact that she had advanced at least $5,000 toward Sarah's legal expenses. Her motives remained unclear until the litigation was concluded. Then her apparent role as mentor was revealed. If she had been, as some believed, the instigator of the Sharon affair; and if she had, as many believed, financed Sarah's litigation, hoping for an equal share of the settlement; then it was no surprise that she signed the papers to commit Sarah Althea to a life sentence in the insane asylum. As a business deal her investment had not produced the expected return and she was canny enough to know when to cut her losses. She never saw Sarah Althea again. She never visited her at the hospital, nor did she even write a single line. In fact, immediately after Sarah's departure Mammy hired an attorney who arranged to have the Terry's Fresno home ransacked for Sarah Althea's silverware, jewelry, and magnificent wardrobe, all of which were delivered to Mammy Pleasant's Octavia Street house in San Francisco.

But, if Terry's death was essentially "the last" for Sarah Althea, Sarah Althea's commitment was essentially "the last" for Mammy Pleasant. She retired into her own comings and goings and was forgotten. She aged, grew ill and died on January 11, 1904, at the age of 89 -- penniless and virtually friendless. She was buried, with her secrets, at Tucolay Cemetery in Napa.

THE MORGAN HILL
RANCH SUBDIVISION

The Morgan Hill Ranch Subdivision

ith the passing of Mammy Pleasant the saga of Sarah Althea was complete and, though the events greatly colored the lives of all participants, those who were merely onlookers were also affected. For Hiram Morgan Hill and Diana the publicity surrounding the six years of litigation involving Hill's sister altered their course significantly. Instead of attending to their ranch in Morgan Hill as planned, they first escaped to Europe and the East and then settled into separated lives, with Hill at the Murphy's Rancho Grande in Halleck, Nevada, and Diana and their daughter in elegant quarters in Washington, D.C. The Hills continued to own the Villa Miramonte home and 200 acres surrounding it until 1912 but it was rented out to local families including the Hollys and the Hales. According to reports in the Morgan Hill Sun-Times the Hills made annual visits to their property but it was undoubtedly in connection with the subdivision of Diana's 4,900 acres of the original 8,927.10 acre Rancho Ojo de Agua de la Coche. To these were added Daniel Murphy Jr.'s more than 4,000 acres.

In 1892 the property was turned over to C.H. Phillips, California's leading land developer, who had been one of the first to create land divisions on the great ranches of San Luis Obispo and Santa

Courtesy Bancroft Library

C.H. Phillips

Colonist Tickets *Will be sold to* California

Via the SOUTHERN PACIFIC

February 12 to April 30, 1901

From Chicago : : : : : : : $30.00
From St. Louis, Memphis or New Orleans : 27.50
From Kansas City, St. Joseph, Omaha, Council
 Bluffs, Sioux City : : : : : 25.00
And at correspondingly low rates from other points

*In selecting a site for your HOME do not over-
look the claims of*

MORGANHILL

Which is 20 miles south of San Jose in Santa Clara County. The soil is well adapted for fruit raising and the acreage planted and orchards coming into bearing are increasing every season. Land can be had for from $20 to $100 an acre, according to situation. The rainfall is sufficient without irrigation, but water is so plentiful from creeks running through the valley that it would be easy to store it for any purpose at any time. The heat of summer is tempered by a sea breeze and the nights are always cool. There is no malaria and the climate is beneficial in rheumatic and lung diseases. The scenery is varied by hill and dale and many magnificent old oak trees. The district has only been opened up since 1892 but there is already a flourishing little town of some hundreds of people with four churches, a good schoolhouse and no saloons. The place may be said to be going ahead at a rate of nearly 30 per cent a year. Being on the main line of the new through coast route the rate of progress will no doubt rapidly increase. There is first-class hunting and fishing and many desirable camping grounds in the vicinity.

*For further information
call on or write the nearest agent of the*

SOUTHERN PACIFIC COMPANY
...OR...

Secret'y Board of Trade, Morganhill

*Flyers such as these were designed to lure midwestern farmers to the riches of California.
They were distributed by the Southern Pacific Railroad.*

Barbara counties before arriving in Santa Clara County. Phillips was seriously considered as a Republican nominee for Governor of the State in the 1890's and he was, in the words of California historian, Hubert Howe Bancroft, "a representative man in the new era of California -- extraordinarily successful in subdividing large areas of land and making them a hundred-fold increased in value."

The subdivision was heralded by the San Jose Mercury newspaper in a special edition devoted to the development of south Santa Clara County. The reader was informed that:

> A division into small parcels of one vast estate has already begun, the famous Morgan Hill tract, and the division of the great San Martin ranch will be commenced in the future.

> ...the fertile Morgan Hill ranch, comprising more than 10,000 acres has been surveyed into small tracts and...a town...plotted. People of moderate means now have the opportunity of getting desirable land and establishing for themselves homes.

Regarding C.H. Phillips' involvement, the writer made this comment:

> Of course, C.H. Phillips was not entirely guided ...by philanthropy when he secured this very desirable property and placed it on the market at one hundred dollars per acre. Mr. Phillips is one of the largest real estate operators in California, and...undoubtedly expects to get a fair return on his investment.

Morgan Hill Ranch.

5,000 ACRES.

In Subdivisions of 5, 10, 20 Acres and Upwards.

TERMS OF SALE:

One-third cash; balance in four equal annual payments, one, two, three and four years; interest 7 per cent per annum. The mortgage tax being paid by the mortgagee, makes the interest less than 6 per cent net to the purchaser. A reasonable deposit will be required in all cases, to cover expenses of making and recording papers.

San Martin Ranch.

10,000 ACRES.

In Subdivisions of 5, 10, 20 Acres and Upwards.

TERMS OF SALE:

One-third cash; balance in four equal annual payments, one, two, three and four years; interest 7½ per cent per annum. The mortgage tax being paid by the mortgagee, makes the interest less than 6 per cent net to the purchaser. A reasonable deposit will be required in all cases, to cover expenses of making and recording papers.

C. H. PHILLIPS.

For full Particulars, Maps, etc., apply at 34 East Santa Clara street, to

L. A. BURBANK.

Advertisement for the Morgan Hill Ranch, The Pioneer, July 15, 1893.

The article continued, tracing the ownership of the land from Daniel Murphy to his daughter, Diana Helen Murphy, "now Mrs. Morgan Hill."

The town was first called Huntington but was changed to Morganhill -- the contracted version evidently intended to separate the person from the place. Advantages of the property included "long stretches of level plains, heavily wooded, with ancient oaks giving the appearance of an English park." And some improvements were promised including curbing, clearing, and leveling of the first four roads, Main Avenue, Diana Avenue, Dunne Avenue, and Hill Road -- "all in all, eight miles of fine driveways shaded by colossal oaks." A perennial water supply was assured by numerous springs and creeks as well as by artesian sources, while the quantity of live and white oak was bringing up to $9 a cord in San Jose. This latter fact was important to settlers who planned on making their $15 a month mortgage payments by cutting and selling oak wood.

In 1906 the number of residents in and around Morganhill Station was sufficient to warrant a petition for incorporation. The benefits listed by the businessmen proponents included economic independence from the county and the establishment of Morganhill as a center of business and agricultural importance. Those opposed to the measure, mostly farmers, prophesied "extravagant expenditures for sidewalks and water systems at the expense of the local taxpayers." However, the sentiment for incorporation prevailed by a vote of 65 to 1 and on November 2, 1906, the settlement that had developed around the home of Diana and Morgan Hill became the City of Morgan Hill.

Newspaper sketch which read, "From the right eminence in the foreground, near the residence of Mr. D.C. Cutting, the artist has shown about 6000 acres of the Morgan Hill Ranch looking from east to west. Main, Diana and Dunne Avenues run parallel to each other through the grove of oaks, with Murphy's Peak and Nob Hill in the background."

References:

For more about the Martin Murphy family consult the following:

Arbuckle, Clyde. *Santa Clara Ranchos*. San Jose: Harlan-Young Press, 1968.

Hunter, Joyce. *In the Shadow of El Toro*. Morgan Hill: Marie Stinnett and James L. Stinnett Jr., 1978.

Sawyer, Eugene T. *History of Santa Clara County, California*. Los Angeles: Historic Record Company, 1922.

Sullivan, Sister Gabrielle. *Martin Murphy Jr., California Pioneer 1844-1884*. Pacific Center for Western Historical Studies. Stockton: University of the Pacific, 1974.

For more about Sarah Althea Hill, William Sharon, David Smith Terry, and Mammy Pleasant consult the following:

Gould, Milton S. *A Cast of Hawks*. La Jolla: Copley Books, 1985.

Holdredge, Helen. *Mammy Pleasant*. San Carlos: Nourse Publishing Company, 1953.

Kroninger, Robert H. *Sarah and the Senator*. Berkeley: Howell-North Press, 1964.

For more about the history of Morgan Hill consult the following:

Beroza, Muriel Nelson. *Sveadal*. Paradise Valley, AZ: Paradise Valley Press, 1976.

Kellogg, Charles. *Charles Kellogg and the Nature Singer. His book*. Morgan Hill: Pacific Science Press, 1930.

Miller, Myron, "A Historical Study of the Development of Rancho Ojo Agua de la Coche." A Thesis presented to the Faculty of the Division of Education at San Jose State College. San Jose, August, 1952.

Sepeda, Delores de Moro. *Hills West of El Toro*. A Story about Uvas Canyon. United States: Braun Brumfield, Inc. 1978.

Wyman, Beth. "The History of Morgan Hill, California. From Indians to Incorporation." A Thesis presented to the Faculty of the Division of History at San Jose State University. San Jose, June 1982.

All of the above are available through the Morgan Hill branch of the Santa Clara County Library. Some are available for purchase at the Morgan Hill Museum and, also, through local bookstores.